AQA PSYCHOLOGY A-LEVEL YEAR 2. TWO A STAR EXAMS. PAPER 1 AND PAPER 2 (FIRST SET).

Full mark answers to 2 Past Papers.

By Joseph Anthony Campbell

First Printing: November 2020.

CONTENTS

AUTHOR'S NOTE.

This book will provide you with crystal clear and accurate examples of 'A' star grade AQA A level Psychology paper examinations from the new syllabus and enables students to achieve the same grade in their upcoming examinations.

I teach both GCSE and A level Psychology and I am a qualified and experienced Psychology teacher and tutor of over 17 years standing. I teach, write and provide independent tuition in Central and West London.

The resources in this book WILL help you get an A or A star in your AQA A level Psychology examinations, as they have done and will continue to do so, for my students.

Best wishes,

Joseph

ABOUT THE AUTHOR.

I graduated from the Universities of Liverpool and Leeds and I obtained first class honours in my teacher training.

I have taught and provided private tuition for over 17 years up to University level. I also write academic resources for the Times Educational Supplement.

My tuition students have been fortunate enough to attain places to study at Oxford, Cambridge and Imperial College, London and other Russell Group Universities. The students have done very well in their examinations and one Psychology student even obtained full UMS marks in her A2 Psychology examination. I hope and know that my Psychology books can enable you to take the next step on your academic journey.

SUMMARY OF THE EXAMINATION PAPERS.

The examinations are linear i.e. they are all done at the end of each year.

There are **2** examination papers for Psychology AS level.

There are **3** examination papers for Psychology A level.

(I have written further books to help you with the AS level and Paper 3 of the A level and I have provided details of the AS level Psychology papers and the Paper 3 A level topics in those Psychology books).

In this book, we are concerned with Paper 1 and Paper 2 of the A level examinations which are completed at the end of your 'A' levels (usually the end of Year 2).

Paper **1** is divided into **4** sections:

Section A - Social Influence

Section B – Memory

Section C – Attachment

Section D - Psychopathology

Each section is worth 24 marks and the paper has a total of 96 marks. There is 2 hours (120 minutes) for the exam (unless you have extra time).

Paper **2** is divided into **3** sections:

Section A – Approaches in Psychology

Section B – Psychopathology

Section C – Research Methods

Section A and B are worth 24 marks and Section C is worth 48 marks. The paper has a total of 96 marks. There is 2 hours (120 minutes) for the exam (unless you have extra time).

Each Paper is worth one third of your total A level Psychology mark.

The exam structure is complicated. In each section there will be multiple choice questions, short answer questions and at least one extended writing question. This is why the examples in this book are particularly useful as you will need to familiarise yourself with these types of questions and their structure for each examination. They range from 1 to 16 marks per question.

AQA A-LEVEL PSYCHOLOGY (7182/1) PAPER 1 INTRODUCTORY TOPICS IN PSYCHOLOGY. SPECIMEN MATERIAL (FIRST SET) 2017

HTTP://FILESTORE.AQA.ORG.UK/RESOURCES/PSYCHOLOGY/AQA-71821-SQP.PDF

SECTION A: SOCIAL INFLUENCE

Answer all questions in this section (24 marks and 30 minutes for each section on Paper 1)

0 1 Which of the following terms best matches the statements below? Choose one term that matches each statement and write A, B, C, D or E in the box next to it. Use each letter once only.

A Identification
B Informational social influence
C Normative social influence
D Compliance
E Internalisation

[4 marks] (5 minutes) (AO1 = 4)

Publicly changing behaviour whilst maintaining a different private view. [1 mark]

D

Group pressure leading to a desire to fit in with the group. [1 mark]

C

When a person lacks knowledge of how to behave and looks to the group for guidance. [1 mark]

B

Conforming to the behaviour of a role model. [1 mark]

A

0 2 Briefly outline and evaluate the findings of any one study of social influence.

[4 marks] (5 minutes) (AO1 = 2; AO3 = 2) (100 words maximum)

Asch placed male participants in an unambiguous situation where the majority of participants conformed at least once when confederates gave the same wrong answer to a question comparing line lengths across various trials. 75% of participants conformed at least once across 18 trials.

(AO1=2)

The study lacks ecological validity however, as whether the participants were right or wrong did not really matter to the participants; they may have been less likely to conform if their answers had real-life consequences. Also, in terms of ethics, the participants were deceived as to the true nature of the study.

(AO3=2)

(95 words)

0 3 Read the item and then answer the question that follows.

Two psychology students were discussing the topic of social influence.

'I find it fascinating how some people are able to resist social influence', said Jack. 'It must be the result of having a confident personality.'

'I disagree', replied Sarah. 'I think resisting social influence depends much more on the presence of others.'

Discuss two explanations of resistance to social influence. As part of your discussion, refer to the views expressed by Jack and Sarah in the conversation above.

[16 marks] (20 minutes) (AO1 = 6; AO2 = 4; AO3 = 6) (400 words maximum)

One explanation of resistance to social influence is that of social support, a situational factor. Sarah states that resistance depends on 'the presence of others' and Milgram found that participants are less likely to obey authority if there were other dissenting confederates present. Asch found similar results in variations of his experiment on conformity in an unambiguous situation when he tested the effect of the participant having a supporter in the group i.e. one of the confederates agreed with the participant. Having a fellow dissenter who disagreed with the majority broke the unanimity of the group. This made it easier for the participant to resist the pressure to conform and the rate of conformity fell to 5.5%. This finding is reflected in Sarah's comment that 'social influence depends much more on the presence of others.'

Jack however suggests that dispositional factors in resisting social influence are more important. Another explanation of resistance is that of 'locus of control'. Jack states that '...how some people are able to resist social influence...must be the result of having a confident personality'. If someone has an internal locus of control, they are more likely to accept personal responsibility for their own actions. They are therefore less likely to obey authoritative demands that are against both their morals and views. If someone has an external locus of control, they are less likely to accept personal responsibility for their actions and are therefore more likely to feel helpless and obedient when confronted with a perceived authority figure. This explanation of resistance to social influence provides an alternative, viable explanation through a dispositional factor as to why people would resist social influence.

However as to the psychological experiments that have provided these two explanations of resistance to social influence, both Asch and Milgram's experiments have been criticised for the deceptive elements of their studies. Asch and Milgram' participants encounter the ethical issue of deception as Asch's participants believed that they were taking part in a study to determine line lengths whilst Milgram's participants believed that the experiment was based on the effects of punishment on learning and that they were actually providing electric shocks to participants. The experiments could have had a long-term impact on the participants and both experiments could therefore lack validity and be criticised for their levels of ecological validity due to the fact that they were both artificial laboratory experiments.

(397 words)

SECTION B: MEMORY

Answer all questions in this section (24 marks and 30 minutes for each section on Paper 1)

Read the item and then answer the questions that follow.

An experiment was carried out to test the effects of learning similar and dissimilar information on participants' ability to remember.

In Stage 1 of the experiment, 10 participants in Group A, the 'similar' condition, were given a list of 20 place names in the UK. They were given two minutes to learn the list. 10 different participants in Group B, the 'dissimilar' condition, were given the same list of 20 place names in the UK. They were also given two minutes to learn the list.

In Stage 2 of the experiment, participants in Group A were given a different list of 20 more place names in the UK, and were given a further two minutes to learn it. Participants in Group B were given a list of 20 boys' names, and were given a further two minutes to learn it.

In Stage 3 of the experiment, all participants were given five minutes to recall as many of the 20 place names in the UK, from the list in Stage 1, as they could. The raw data from the two groups is below.

Table 1: Number of place names recalled from the list in Stage 1.

Group A	*Group B*
5	*11*
6	*10*
4	*11*
7	*13*
8	*12*
4	*14*
5	*15*
4	*11*
6	*14*
7	*14*

0 4-0 1 What is the most appropriate measure of central tendency for calculating the average of the scores, from Table 1, in each of the two groups? Justify your answer.

[2 marks] (2.5 minutes) (AO2 = 2) (50 words maximum)

The mean is the appropriate measure of central tendency for calculating the average of the scores. The mean is the most sensitive method as it takes all the scores in each data set into account.

(35 words)

0 4-0 2 Calculate the measure of central tendency you have identified in your answer to question 04.0 1 for Group A and Group B. Show your calculations for each group.

[4 marks] (5 minutes) (AO2 = 4)

5+6+4+7+8+4+5+4+6+7=56/10= 5.6 = Group A mean
11+10+11+13+12+14+15+11+14+14=125/10= 12.5 =Group B mean

0 4-0 3 In Stage 3 of the experiment, several participants in Group A, the 'similar' condition, recalled words from the Stage 2 list rather than the Stage 1 list.

Use your knowledge of forgetting to explain why this may have occurred.

[2 marks] (2.5 minutes) (AO2 = 2) (50 words maximum)

The information presented in Stage 1 and Stage 2 was similar and the new information disrupted/interfered with the recall of previous information. This is called retroactive interference.

(27 words)

0 5 Describe and evaluate the working memory model of memory.

[16 marks] (20 minutes) (AO1 = 6; AO3 = 10) (400 words maximum)

The working memory model (WMM) was created by Baddeley and Hitch in 1974 and the model proposed that short term memory was comprised of three different stores; the phonological loop, the episodic buffer and the visuo-spatial sketchpad. The central executive receives all of the information that is paid attention to (attentional focus) and directs the information to one of the three slave systems according to its type. Speech-based information is directed to the phonological loop; visual and spatial information is directed towards the visuo-spatial sketchpad and the episodic buffer (2000) stores information from the other two slave systems and integrates the information together to form episodes along with information from long term memory (LTM) in order to make complete scenes or form 'episodes. All of the slave systems have limited capacity and duration and therefore in order to store information for a long time, information must be passed on to the long-term memory.

The working memory model is supported by evidence such as the case study of KF by Shallice and Washington (1974). KF sustained brain damage in a motorbike accident and had problems with certain areas of short-term memory. KF could recall and process visual information but had trouble recalling words verbally. This suggests that he had an impaired articulatory loop but an intact visuo-spatial sketchpad. KF's condition could not be explained by the multi-store model of memory (MSM) which delineates short term memory as one store and in the case of KF it instead supports the working memory model's theory that short-term memory is made up of multiple stores and an active processor unlike the multi-store model of memory which contains a discrete store only.

The working memory model also does not place as much emphasis on rehearsal as the multi-store model. Rehearsal is only one possible process in the working memory model which helps to explain how information enters the long-term memory after little or no rehearsal. This means that the working memory model allows for other explanations on processes rather than one finite explanation as provided by the multi-store model.

However, some psychologists argue that the central executive is too vague and simplistic in its description; it is merely described as 'attention' in the working memory model. The central executive concept is also not supported as it is extremely difficult to design tasks to test it and therefore there is little empirical evidence for its existence.

(400 words)

SECTION C: ATTACHMENT

Answer all questions in this section (24 marks and 30 minutes for each section on Paper 1)

06 Name three stages in the development of attachments identified by Schaffer.

[3 marks] (3.75 minutes) (AO1 = 3)

1 Pre-attachment (Asocial)
2 Indiscriminate (Multiple)
3 Discriminate (Single)

07 Read the item and then answer the question that follows.

A nursery school worker and her manager were chatting at the end of the day.

'How did the new toddlers settle in today?' asked the manager.

'They behaved very differently', replied the nursery school worker. 'Max was distressed when his mother left but was happy to see her at the end of the day.'

'Jessica arrived clinging to her mother and I could not calm her down when her mother left.'

'William barely seemed to notice when his mother left and did not even look up when she returned to collect him.'

Name the attachment type demonstrated by each of the children in the conversation above by writing the attachment type next to the name below.

[3 marks] (3.75 minutes) (AO2 = 3)

Max	Secure
Jessica	Insecure - resistant
William	Insecure - avoidant

0 8 Briefly evaluate learning theory as an explanation of attachment.

[4 marks] (5 minutes) (AO3 = 4) (100 words maximum)

Support for learning theory is derived from scientific research involving research on animals. This is a limitation because it presents the problem of anthropomorphic extrapolation because it is not possible to fully extrapolate from animals to humans as humans and animals are inherently different. It is also difficult to tell in learning theory if an association has taken place and if it ever will take place when studying babies in their early months. For example, Schaffer and Emerson (1964) found that many babies did not have their mother as the primary attachment figure despite the mother being the primary caregiver.

(100 words)

0 9 Read the item and then answer the question that follows.

A group of researchers used 'event sampling' to observe children's friendships over a period of three weeks at break times and lunchtimes during the school day.

Explain what is meant by 'event sampling'.

[2 marks] (2.5 minutes) (AO1 = 2) (50 words maximum)

'Event sampling' is when researchers comprise a list of events they want to study (e.g. holding hands, speaking aloud) and compile a period of time in which to record said events (e.g. 5 hourly periods). The researchers then record the events that occur in the period of time previously designated.

(50 words)

1 0 The investigation in question 09 is an example of a 'naturalistic observation'. Briefly discuss how observational research might be improved by conducting observations in a controlled environment.

[4 marks] (5 minutes) (AO3 = 4) (100 words maximum)

Controlled environments such as laboratory experiments offer a strong level of control of extraneous variables during observational research. Extraneous variables can interfere or affect the results of the observational research. The removal or minimising of said extraneous variables makes it easier to both establish a causal relationship between the independent and dependent variable and for a later researcher to conduct the same experiment/observation and replicate the same results. This increases both the reliability and the validity of the observational research which could be improved by conducting observations in a controlled environment.

(91 words)

11 Discuss research into the influence of early attachment on adult relationships.

[8 marks] (10 minutes) (AO1 = 4; AO3 = 4) (200 words maximum)

Hazan and Shaver (1987) conducted a 'love quiz' in a local newspaper. The quiz assessed the attachment type (secure, insecure resistant or insecure avoidant) between participants and their parents. The other section assessed their current beliefs about romantic love. The first 620 responses were analysed and secure children tended to have fully functional, trusting relationships; insecure resistant children were more likely to be extremely worried that they were not loved in their relationships and insecure avoidant children tended to fear intimacy. This provides support for Bowlby's theory that adult relationships are influenced by early attachment.

However, Freud and Dann (1951) provided evidence that those early attachments may not have as large an effect on adult relationships as Hazan and Shaver's (1987) results implied. They studied 6 children who were orphaned during World War Two and raised in a deportation camp. They were unable to form any adult attachments. However, when the children grew up, they developed average intelligence and were able to form fully functioning relationships. Freud and Dann concluded that this was because they had formed attachments amongst themselves as children. This offers an alternative interpretation of a viable early attachment and its influence on later adult relationships.

(199 words)

SECTION D: PSYCHOPATHOLOGY

Answer all questions in this section (24 marks and 30 minutes for each section on Paper 1)

1 2 Which two of the following are examples of Jahoda's criteria for 'ideal mental health'? Shade two boxes only. For each answer completely fill in the circle alongside the appropriate answer.

[2 marks] (2.5 minutes) (AO1 = 2)

A Dependence on others
B Environmental mastery SHADE THIS BOX
C Lack of inhibition
D Maladaptiveness
E Resistance to stress SHADE THIS BOX

1 3 Read the item and then answer the question that follows.

The following article appeared in a magazine:

Hoarding disorder – A 'new' mental illness

Most of us are able to throw away the things we don't need on a daily basis. Approximately 1 in 1000 people, however, suffer from hoarding disorder, defined as

'a difficulty parting with items and possessions, which leads to severe anxiety and extreme clutter that affects living or work spaces'.

Apart from 'deviation from ideal mental health', outline three definitions of abnormality. Refer to the article above in your answer.

[6 marks] (7.5 minutes) (AO1 = 3; AO2 = 3) (150 words maximum)

One definition of abnormality is a deviation from statistical norms. Behaviour that is rare statistically is considered abnormal within this approach (people on the tail ends of a bell curve graph are statistically rare and therefore abnormal). People with 'hoarding disorder' are '1 in 1000 people', they are therefore statistically rare and abnormal.

Another definition of abnormality is an individual being unable to function adequately. Criteria for diagnosis include dysfunctional behaviour (behaviour which contrasts with the cultures accepted and expected behaviour) and personal distress (the individual is excessively emotional). In this case, the 'hoarding disorder' is causing the sufferers, 'severe anxiety'.

Deviation from social norms is a third definition of abnormality. This outlines an individual who contrasts with the expected and accepted behaviours of their society (the social norms). As the article states 'Most of us are able to throw away the things we don't need on a daily basis'.

(150 words)

1 4 Read the item and then answer the question that follows.

Kirsty is in her twenties and has had a phobia of balloons since one burst near her face when she was a little girl. Loud noises such as 'banging' and 'popping' cause Kirsty extreme anxiety, and she avoids situations such as birthday parties and weddings, where there might be balloons.

Suggest how the behavioural approach might be used to explain Kirsty's phobia of balloons.

[4 marks] (5 minutes) (AO2 = 4) (100 words maximum)

The behavioural approach may explain Kirsty's phobia of balloons as a product of classical conditioning i.e. Kirsty has learnt to associate balloons with fear. This means that a neutral stimulus (NS) (a balloon) has been presented with an unconditioned stimulus (UCS-loud noise) and produced an unconditioned response (UCR-fear). In this way balloons inspire and cause a response of fear in Kirsty. This fear has been maintained through operant conditioning as Kirsty's avoidance of situations where there might be balloons has prevented this conditioned anxiety and fear (CR-fear) from occurring (negative reinforcement). Thus, she may continually repeat this avoidant behaviour.

(99 words)

1 5 Read the item and then answer the questions that follow.

Twenty depressed patients were treated using cognitive behavioural therapy. Over the course of the six-week treatment, each patient's mood was monitored every week using a self-report mood scale (where a score of 20 = extremely positive mood and a score of 0 = extremely negative mood). Each week they also completed a quality of sleep questionnaire which was scored from 10 = excellent sleep to 0 = very poor sleep.

At the end of the study the researchers correlated each patient's final mood score with his or her final sleep score.

1 5-0 2 Outline one way in which the researchers should have dealt with ethical issues in this study.

[2 marks] (2.5 minutes) (AO3 = 2) (50 words maximum)

The researchers should have constantly offered or made the participants aware of the right for them to withdraw from the study. This would prevent participant discomfort and distress.

(28 words)

1 5-0 3 The sleep questionnaire used by the researchers had not been checked to see whether or not it was a reliable measure of sleep quality.

Explain how this study could be modified by checking the sleep questionnaire for test-retest reliability.

[4 marks] (5 minutes) (AO3 = 4) (100 words maximum)

This would be achieved by modifying the sleep questionnaire for test-retest reliability. Firstly, the participants would complete the sleep questionnaire more than once. The scores would then be correlated from each questionnaire. A scatter graph would also be used and on one axis the first tests results and, on another axis, the later test's results. This would then be assessed using a Spearman's Rho test and the reliability is then determined by comparing the correlation with the statistical table. It would be expected to display a strong, positive correlation between the two sets of scores.

(95 words)

1 6 Outline cognitive behaviour therapy as a treatment for depression.

[4 marks] (5 minutes) (AO1 = 4) (100 words maximum)

Cognitive behavioural therapy (CBT) attempts to identify and rectify the patient's faulty cognitions. There are many ways that the therapist and patient can do this. The therapist tries to help the client discern that these cognitions are faulty by questioning them and focusing upon the clients' successes in life. The client may be encouraged to keep a diary to help them become more aware of their thoughts and feelings. The therapy aims to mostly focus on what the client's personal situation is but the therapist may also draw on the client's past experiences.

(93 words)

AQA A-LEVEL PSYCHOLOGY (7182/2) PAPER 2 PSYCHOLOGY IN CONTEXT SPECIMEN MATERIAL (FIRST SET) 2017

HTTP://FILESTORE.AQA.ORG.UK/RESOURCES/PSYCHOLOGY/AQA-71822-SQP.PDF

SECTION A: APPROACHES IN PSYCHOLOGY

Answer all questions in this section (24 marks and 30 minutes for this section)

0 1 Which one of the following statements is false? Shade one box only.

[1 mark] (1.25 minutes) (AO1 = 1)

A Repression can lead to unpleasant memories causing distress
B Repression causes people to have difficulty accessing unpleasant memories
C Repression involves people choosing to forget unpleasant memories SHADE THIS BOX
D Repression involves unpleasant memories being kept from conscious awareness

0 1-0 2 Which one of the following statements is false? Shade one box only.

[1 mark] (1.25 minutes) (AO1 = 1)

A The Id is responsible for pleasure-seeking behaviour
B The Id is responsible for unreasonable behaviour
C The Superego is responsible for bad behaviour SHADE THIS BOX
D The Superego is responsible for guilty feelings

0 2 Read the item and then answer the question that follows.

In a laboratory study of problem-solving, cognitive psychologists asked participants to solve problems presented in different colours of ink. They found that it took longer to solve problems presented in green ink, than it did to solve problems presented in other colours. They inferred that the mental processing of problems is made more difficult when a problem is presented in green ink.

Explain what is meant by 'inference' in relation to this study.

[2 marks] (2.5 minutes) (AO2 = 2) (50 words maximum)

Inference refers to assumptions made about mental processes that are not directly supported by evidence. In this context, the psychologists are inferring that because the green ink questions seemingly made the participants solve the problems at a slower rate that they then had more difficulty actually mentally processing the problems.

(50 words)

0 3 Read the item and then answer the question that follows.

Dominic is unhappy and lacks confidence. He also thinks he is not very good-looking and not very clever. He goes to a counselling therapist for help. The therapist suggests that Dominic lacks congruence.

Outline what is meant by 'congruence'. Explain one way in which Dominic might achieve 'congruence'.

[4 marks] (5 minutes) (AO1 = 2; AO2 = 2) (100 words maximum)

Congruence is the difference between the self as known to the individual and the self the person aspires to become. The therapist could endeavour to bridge the gap between the two incongruent aspects of this self for Dominic by helping him to be able to assess himself more accurately. Through the therapist offering Dominic unconditional positive regard (UPR), Dominic could achieve a more realistic view of himself.

(67 words)

0 4 Discuss the contribution of behaviourist psychologists such as Pavlov and Skinner to our understanding of human behaviour.

[16 marks] (20 minutes) (AO1 = 6; AO3 = 10) (400 words maximum)

Ivan Pavlov carried out an experiment whereby he rang a bell and then provided dogs with food immediately afterwards. The dogs began to associate the bell with food through repetition and soon the bell alone caused salivation. The food was an unconditioned stimulus that produced an unconditioned response (salivation). When the unconditioned stimulus was repeatedly presented with a neutral stimulus (the bell), it was associated with the unconditioned stimulus (the food) and produced a now conditioned response (salivation) and thus became a conditioned stimulus. Pavlov labelled this classical conditioning and it later became known as Pavlovian conditioning.

B.F. Skinner studied how animals and by extension, humans, learn from the consequences of their actions – in particular through positive and negative reinforcement. Positive reinforcement is when something desirable is obtained through the subject partaking in a particular behaviour and Skinner's experiments on rats display this as rats were conditioned to press a lever because it provided them with food, which was desirable. Negative reinforcement describes an undesirable experience or item being removed as a consequence of a particular behaviour and the rats also learnt to press a lever to prevent an electric shock. Skinner labelled this as operant conditioning.

However, although conditioning is supported by evidence, it cannot explain all behaviour. Animals and humans can also learn through observation as demonstrated by the social learning theory. This means that Skinner and Pavlov's theories into conditioning cannot be used on their own to explain all behaviour.

Both Pavlov and Skinner's experiments and much behaviourist evidence relies on animal research. This means that there is a problem of anthropomorphic extrapolation as humans and animals are inherently different in both morals and physicality. Therefore, there is a problem of relating animal studies to humans. Behaviourists seemingly ignore genetic factors also which can impact what different species can learn through conditioning.

Behaviourists also fail to take into account abstract concepts such as morals and also state the 'mind' is irrelevant. Both Skinner and Pavlov fail to outline cognitive processes that take place during conditioning and therefore provide an incomplete explanation of behaviour. It has been applied to classrooms in education and various modes of therapy however and applicability has been found in relation to the real world and it has been useful in understanding certain aspects of human behaviour.

(383 words)

SECTION B: BIOPSYCHOLOGY

Answer all questions in this section (24 marks and 30 minutes for this section)

0 6 The electroencephalogram (EEG) and event-related potentials (ERPs) both involve recording the electrical activity of the brain.

Outline one difference between the EEG and ERPs.

[2 marks] (2.5 minutes) (AO2 = 2) (50 words maximum)

EEG's show the overall electrical activity in the brain, meaning that it is often used to study sleep patterns.

ERP'S, however, display changes in EEG wave patterns in response to a stimulus, to link certain stimuli to certain responses.

(39 words)

0 7 Read the item and then answer the question that follows.

Sam is a police officer. She has just started working the night shift and after a week, she finds that she has difficulty sleeping during the day and is becoming tense and irritable. Sam is also worried that she is less alert during the night shift itself.

Using your knowledge of endogenous pacemakers and exogenous zeitgebers, explain Sam's experiences.

[4 marks] (5 minutes) (AO2 = 4) (100 words maximum)

Due to the fact that Sam has been on the night shift for a week her endogenous pacemaker or internal biological clock is out of sync with the exogenous zeitgeber of light. This is because she has to remain awake at night when it is dark and sleep during the day when it is light. This disruption in her sleep-wake cycle has been linked to the problem Sam is experiencing such as difficulty in sleeping and therefore feeling tense and irritable.

(81 words)

0 8 The human female menstrual cycle is an example of one type of biological rhythm; it is called a:

A circadian rhythm
B infradian rhythm
C ultradian rhythm

[1 mark] (1.25 minutes) (AO1 = 1)

B

0 9 Outline the structures and processes involved in synaptic transmission.

[6 marks] (7.5 minutes) (AO1 = 6) (150 words maximum)

When an electrical impulse reaches the end of a neuron, neurotransmitters are released into the synaptic cleft, which diffuse to the postsynaptic membrane. These neurotransmitters might trigger an electric pulse down the postsynaptic membrane therefore continuing through to the synaptic cleft. After the neurotransmitters trigger the electric pulse they are reabsorbed by the presynaptic neuron or broken down by enzymes.

Synaptic transmission occurs at the junction between two neurons. The receptors are on the postsynaptic membranes, which means that the impulses are unidirectional. Excitatory neurotransmitters (e.g. Acetylcholine) make it more likely that an electrical impulse in the postsynaptic neuron will be triggered. Inhibitory neurotransmitters such as gamma-Aminobutyric acid (GABA) make it less likely that an electrical impulse will be triggered in the postsynaptic neuron.

(126 words)

1 0 Split brain patients show unusual behaviour when tested in experiments. Briefly explain how unusual behaviour in split brain patients could be tested in an experiment.

[2 marks] (2.5 minutes) (AO2 = 2) (50 words maximum)

Participants who have had split brain surgery could split their visual field by covering one of their eyes in two conditions in a repeated measures experiment and when shown a word or a picture they could report or attempt to draw what they see.

(44 words)

1 1 Briefly evaluate research using split brain patients to investigate hemispheric lateralisation of function.

[4 marks] (5 minutes) (AO3 = 4) (100 words maximum)

Results found in split brain research cannot always be accurately generalised in order to create nomothetic theories due to their small sample size (e.g. Sperry used only 11 participants). Therefore, the findings do not allow for anomalies and have little practical use. Also, the findings of split-brain patients whom had had drug treatment were compared to an epileptic control group that had not experienced medical (drug) treatment or experienced epilepsy. Therefore, you cannot establish causal relationships when investigating hemispheric lateralisation of function between both splitting the brain and impaired function as impaired function may be due to the medication beforehand.

(100 words)

SECTION C: RESEARCH METHODS

Answer all questions in this section (48 marks and 60 minutes for this section)

Read the item and then answer the questions that follow.

A psychologist wanted to see if verbal fluency is affected by whether people think they are presenting information to a small group of people or to a large group of people.

The psychologist needed a stratified sample of 20 people. She obtained the sample from a company employing 60 men and 40 women.

The participants were told that they would be placed in a booth where they would read out an article about the life of a famous author to an audience. Participants were also told that the audience would not be present, but would only be able to hear them and would not be able to interact with them.

There were two conditions in the study, Condition A and Condition B.

Condition A: 10 participants were told the audience consisted of 5 listeners.
Condition B: the other 10 participants were told the audience consisted of 100 listeners.

Each participant completed the study individually. The psychologist recorded each presentation and then counted the number of verbal errors made by each participant.

1 2 Identify the dependent variable in this study.

[2 marks] (2.5 minutes) (AO2 = 2) (50 words maximum)

The dependent variable is the verbal fluency of the participants, which could be measured by the number of verbal errors they make.

(22 words)

1 3 Write a suitable hypothesis for this study.

[3 marks] (3.75 minutes) (AO2 = 3) (75 words maximum)

There is no difference in the number of verbal errors made by participants who believe they are reading to a small audience (5 listeners) and by participants who believe they are reading to a large audience (100 listeners).

(38 words)

1 4 Identify one extraneous variable that the psychologist should have controlled in the study and explain why it should have been controlled.

[3 marks] (3.75 minutes) (AO2 = 3) (75 words maximum)

It would be important to control the participant's level of familiarity with the famous author as increased levels of familiarity could decrease the number of verbal errors. This uncontrolled participant variable could affect the dependent variable (DV –verbal error rate) rather than the independent variable.

(45 words)

1 5 Explain one advantage of using a stratified sample of participants in this study.

[2 marks] (2.5 minutes) (AO2 = 2) (50 words maximum)

Stratified sampling can produce a representative sample of the group you are attempting to generalise the results to. This means that the results may have a higher level of validity when generalising to the general population as different genders male/female are represented in this study sample in the correct proportions.

(50 words)

1 6 Explain how the psychologist would have obtained the male participants for her stratified sample. Show your calculations.

[3 marks] (3.75 minutes) (AO2 = 3) (75 words maximum)

60% of the 20 participants should be male therefore: (60/100 x 20 = 12.)
12 participants should be male.
Place the names of 60 males written on a piece of paper in a hat and pick names from the hat until you have withdrawn 12 names. These 12 names are the men that will be used in the sample. Then determine the proportion of males needed to mirror the number of males in the target population as follows i.e. 60%.

(75 words)

1 7 The psychologist wanted to randomly allocate the 20 people in her stratified sample to the two conditions. She needed an equal number of males in each condition and an equal number of females in each condition. Explain how she would have done this.

[4 marks] (5 minutes) (AO2 = 4) (100 words maximum)

Firstly, the psychologist must write down all the names of the females on slips of paper and put them in a hat. Then the psychologist must randomly withdraw 4 names and put them in condition 1 and then withdraw 4 names and put them in condition 2. The psychologist then must write down all the names of the males on slips of paper and put them in a different hat and withdraw 6 names out of the hat. These will be the participants in condition 1. Then the psychologist must withdraw another 6 names and put them in condition 2.

(100 words)

1 8 Read the item and then answer the questions that follow.

The results of the study are given in Table 1.

Table 1: Mean number of verbal errors and standard deviations for both conditions

	Condition A (believed audience of 5 listeners)	***Condition B (believed audience of 100 listeners)***
Mean	11.1	17.2
Standard deviation	1.30	3.54

What conclusions might the psychologist draw from the data in Table 1? Refer to the means and standard deviations in your answer.

[6 marks] (7.5 minutes) (AO2 = 2; AO3 = 4) (150 words maximum)

Firstly, the psychologist might conclude that more verbal errors are made when the person believes that they are presenting and reading to a large audience of 100 listeners than if they believe that they are reading to a small audience of 5 listeners. This conclusion is supported by the results of the mean as those in Condition B (believed an audience of 100 listeners) made an average of 17.2 verbal errors whereas those in Condition A (believed an audience of 5 listeners) made an average of 11.1 verbal errors. The psychologist might also conclude that the differences in participants public speaking skills and anxiety levels became more apparent when participants believed that they were presenting to a larger audience as the standard deviation was larger (3.54) in Condition B (believed an audience of 100 listeners) compared to Condition A (believed an audience of 5 listeners) (1.30).

(146 words)

1 9 Read the item and then answer the question that follows.

The psychologist had initially intended to use the range as a measure of dispersion in this study but found that one person in Condition A had made an exceptionally low number of verbal errors.

Explain how using the standard deviation rather than the range in this situation, would improve the study.

[3 marks] (3.75 minutes) (AO3 = 3) (75 words maximum)

The range can be easily affected by one anomalous result meaning that the range is easily affected by errors. In contrast, standard deviation measures the average distance of the scores from the mean not just the difference between the highest verbal error score and the lowest verbal error score and is therefore less easily distorted by a single anomalous or extreme score.

(62 words)

2 0 Name an appropriate statistical test that could be used to analyse the number of verbal errors in Table 1. Explain why the test you have chosen would be a suitable test in this case.

[4 marks] (5 minutes) (AO2 = 4) (100 words maximum)

An unrelated t – test could be used if we record results as interval data (i.e. one verbal error is recorded in the same fashion as another verbal error). The study is also an independent groups design and the psychologist is looking for a difference between the two conditions. All of these factors suggest that the unrelated t-test could be used.

(60 words)

2 1 The psychologist found the results were significant at $p<0.05$. What is meant by 'the results were significant at $p <0.05$'?

[2 marks] (2.5 minutes) (AO1 = 2) (50 words maximum)

This means that the researchers would have a 95% confidence level that the results are significant (i.e. the change in the independent variable is the cause of a change in the dependent variable).

(33 words)

2 2 Briefly explain <u>one</u> method the psychologist could use to check the validity of the data she collected in this study.

[2 marks] (2.5 minutes) (AO2 = 2) (50 words maximum)

They would make the participants take part in a different, established verbal fluency test and check to see that the results from both tests are consistent with one another and positively correlated (concurrent validity).

(34 words)

2 3 Briefly explain one reason why it is important for research to undergo a peer review process.

[2 marks] (2.5 minutes) (AO3 = 2) (50 words maximum)

The peers can check to make sure that not only are the researchers results valid but that the researcher's conclusion/s are supported by their results. This would ensure that the research is less likely to contain any errors when published as it has been independently, objectively scrutinised by peers.

(49 words)

2 4 Read the item and then answer the question that follows.

"The psychologist focused on fluency in spoken communication in her study. Other research has investigated sex differences in non-verbal behaviours such as body language and gestures."

Design an observation study to investigate sex differences in non-verbal behaviour of males and females when they are giving a presentation to an audience.

In your answer you should provide details of:

- ***the task for the participants***
- ***the behavioural categories to be used and how the data will be recorded***
- ***how reliability of the data collection might be established***
- ***ethical issues to be considered.***

[12 marks] (15 minutes) (AO2 = 12) (300 words maximum)

The participants should give an approximately 10-minute individual presentation to an audience from a script such as 'a list of favourite hobbies' that the psychologists have given them 20 minutes before the task, in order to ensure that they have 20 minutes rehearsal time. The psychologists will record the participants' physical language/non-verbal behaviours and then compare the results of the males with the results of the females in order to attempt to find a difference between each gender as regards non-verbal behaviour. The psychologists should record the participants' behaviour using event sampling. Types of non-verbal behaviour must be decided upon and categorised before the study i.e. crossing arms, hand gestures, shifting feet etc. Each time a participant displays one of these behaviours it would then be recorded on a recording sheet.

The reliability of the data collection could be established by using two psychologists to record and closely observe the data and then checking the inter-rater (observer) reliability between them. Inter-rater reliability determines the levels of concordance between each recorders' results and the higher the concordance rate the higher the reliability. A good level of inter-rater reliability is considered to be 80% and anything below this would therefore be considered to have low levels of reliability. Through comparing the separate recordings, we could ensure that we can make a statistical comparison of both raters.

Certain ethical considerations must also be taken into account. The participants must be aware of their right to withdraw, have given their informed consent to take part in the study and they must not be entirely deceived as to what the study is researching. These ethical considerations must be in place in order to protect the psychological welfare of the participants and to ensure that they are protected from physical and psychological harm during the study.

(300 words)

ASSESSMENT OBJECTIVES.

There are three assessment objectives assessed in each examination: **AO1, AO2** and **AO3.**

AO1 = Outline. This involves outlining your knowledge and understanding. It involves recalling and describing theories, studies and methods.

AO2 = Apply. This involves applying your knowledge and understanding. You must apply your knowledge to different situations and contexts. You will apply this from the information given in the text provided in the question; which will be a theoretical or practical example.

AO3 = Evaluate. This involves analysing and interpreting.
Evaluating studies and theories or drawing conclusions.

There may be one, two or all (only in the extended writing questions) of the assessment objectives in each question. Therefore, it is vitally important to be aware of the structure of how the assessment objectives are allocated in each question of the exam in order to maximise your opportunities to obtain full marks in each question.

It is worth noting that **the Assessment Objectives that are to be met for each question are not provided in the examination itself**, which provides a further complication for you. However, I have provided which assessment objectives are being assessed in the practice questions in this book to give you more awareness of what each type of question is looking for in the answer.

Additional points to remember.

1) When you are answering the A02 application section of the question, write 'In terms of application' before providing your AO2 points and give a quotation if possible, particularly if the question is asking you to 'refer' back to the information provided. Also, when you are answering the A03 evaluation section of the question, write 'In terms of evaluation' before providing your AO3 points.

2) Generally, my students prefer to separate the AO's out in their answers i.e. for a 12 mark (AO1 = 6; A03 =6) answer they will write 2 paragraphs with the first paragraph being AO1 (6 marks) and then the second paragraph being AO3 (6 marks) or 4 paragraphs with 3 marks of AO1 or A03 in each paragraph.

TIMINGS.

Please allocate minutes per mark! In the Psychology AQA A level examination Papers 1 and 2; there are 96 marks to aim for in 120 minutes; which works out at **1.25 minutes per mark**. (This is the same minutes per mark as in all your AS and A level Papers). Therefore, **if a question is worth 8 marks then you would spend roughly 10 minutes** on this question. In the examples in this book I have given you the maximum amount of time allowed for each question which always works out at **1.25 minutes per mark.**

A good rule of thumb is to apply the principle that you get **1 mark per correct point made in your answer** i.e. 4 good points for a 4-mark question. My students find that 1 mark per sentence also helps them to apply this rule generally. Similar to all the principles in this book, **you must apply and follow the correct timings for each question and stick to them throughout your exam to get an A or A star in your Psychology examinations.**

If you have extra time allocated to you, just change the calculation to accommodate the extra time you have for each mark i.e. approximately 1.5 minutes per mark if you have 25% extra time and 1.8 minutes per mark if you have 50% extra time. Allocate within your time management the time for checking if you wish but **move on from the set question as soon as you have reached or are coming towards your time limit**. This ensures that you have excellent coverage of your whole exam and therefore attain a very good mark.

Without applying this principle in these examinations (and to a large extent all examinations) you cannot achieve the highest marks! **Apply all of the principles provided in this book to succeed!**

Additional points to remember.

1) **10% of your examination will be composed of mathematical questions**. But please do not be overly concerned, it is only GCSE level Mathematics and involves basic arithmetic, data and graphs.

2) **Approximately a third of all questions at AS and A level Psychology will involve Research Methods** and they can occur in any paper or section of your examination, not just in the Research Methods section. **Please make sure you apply a strong focus to Research Methods in your revision** and remember again that the Mathematics involved is only set at a GCSE level of difficulty.

APPROXIMATE WORD COUNT PER MARK IN PSYCHOLOGY.

Now that you know what is on each examination, how the assessment objectives are assessed and the time allocated for each type of question we come to what would be considered the correct word count per mark for each question. The primary principle though is to spend the right amount of time on each question as mentioned on the previous pages.

Unfortunately, there is no exact rule here as some questions are mathematical and do not require words whilst extended writing questions and essays tend to follow the set word count below more exactly.

In the answers in this book, I have provided the maximum word count for each answer which works out at **25 words per mark**. However, a good rule of thumb is between **15 and 25 words**.

15 words per mark - minimum word count.

20 words per mark – a generally good word count per mark.

25 words per mark – **The maximum word count generally able to be produced, in the time allocated.**

Additional points to remember.

1) If your answer has quality, 25 words per mark gives you the best chance of obtaining the highest marks in your Psychology exam. Obviously, it does not if you are waffling however. (Please remember to answer the question set and to move on in the time allocated.)

2) Generally, Research Methods questions tend to need less words per mark but there are exceptions to this rule.

3) Remember: **Apply the principle that you get 1 mark per correct point made in your answer and 1 mark per sentence also helps to apply this rule** and if you are concise you can obtain each mark in 15 words of writing. I am aware that some students can write faster than others but all should be able to write 15 words per mark at A level in 1.25 minutes (if they have not been allocated extra time). This is where conciseness is important. However, using the principle of one point per sentence: **Each point/sentence and therefore mark should generally be between 15 and 25 words and completed in 1.25 minutes.**

4) My students have applied all the techniques I am providing you with to gain A's and A stars in their Psychology examinations. You can replicate them by following the advice in this book.

SIX FURTHER STEPS TO EXAMINATION SUCCESS!

To gain confidence, we must work hard to gain a strong sense of self confidence. In order to ensure we are able to do this; following the 6 points below is key. These 6 points have been worked out through the process of preparing thousands of students for examination success.

1. **Revise your subjects consistently and look up all of the words you do not understand in a dictionary, on a Kindle or through online search engines. This will ensure that you use the appropriate specialist vocabulary required by your subject in your examination.**

2. **Quality over quantity. Only write that which is very good. Never make a point you are not sure of and always come across as confident to the examiner.**

3. **Relax and believe; this breeds confidence.**

4. **Answer the question that is set. Do not answer the question you wish was on the examination and please do not waffle. Write your points and move on. Short sentences are often better and use paragraphs. If you are not sure what you are writing, please stop! Honesty is confidence;**

waffling is dishonest writing. Your writing is part of who you are; please make sure that it reflects who you are accurately and fully. That it is of the highest standard.

5. **Now that you know what is on each examination, how the assessment objectives are assessed, the time allocated for each type of question and what would be considered the correct word count per mark for each question; remember the primary principle:** ***To spend the right amount of time on each question*** **(needs to be mentioned twice).**

6. **Relax and believe (also needs to be mentioned twice). If you do the above, you will believe in yourself. You will not be nervous; you will believe and you will do well. No one is expecting you to write the most words ever written or to create a new way of thinking, please just write what you know and write it well in the time allocated and you will do very well. This also takes the pressure off you.**

Always work hard; giving your best in a relaxed way. This leads to focus and, "Tachypsychia"- which is a speeding up of the mind which makes time appear to slow down and gives ease, comfort and quality to whatever it is that you are doing (in this case a Psychology exam).

HOW TO SUCCEED IN AN INTERVIEW!

You may have an interview in order to secure an offer from your University of choice; therefore, I have included this article I wrote as regards succeeding in an interview. The information here applies to academic or job interviews and it will give you both the best chance of succeeding and significantly reduce any tension you feel as regards interviews if you follow the simple principles outlined below.

"When we have tasks, we can feel overwhelmed and I use the metaphor of cutting down a tree to describe this. At first, the whole tree seems overwhelming but as you begin to cut it down you feel differently. *You do not begin to feel differently when the tree is cut down but as soon as you start to cut it.* Therefore, just do the next right thing, work within compartments of an hour by hour basis. It is the anticipation of an event that gives us fear that is worse than the event itself. *Perhaps during but definitely after your interview, I promise you, you will feel better.*

Preparation is important and being calm and going to the interview feeling relaxed (as much as is possible) is important. Have the clothes on that you feel good in and *get to the interview with plenty of time to spare;* this is really important! Also aim to sleep as well as you can the night before the interview but accept it calmly if you are unable to.

Everyone is in the same boat as you. All the other people who are being interviewed are nervous too. The interviewers want to see someone good! You are good! Sometimes, in these situations I have feared secretly that I wasn't good enough. However, the interviewers are good and you are good! There is nothing to hide, you can enjoy this, honest! It is a chance to show people what you would like to do if you worked/studied with them. If they asked you for an interview, they already like you. At the end of the interview, if you still want the place/position say, "I want to re-state my interest in working here/being a student at this University. Thank you". However only say this if you mean it. Remember you are interviewing them too; they want a good employee and/or student also. Remember there is nothing more similar to us, which we can relate to more, than another human being. They are all human!

If you have a panel interview this may perhaps be the hardest part of the day; but not necessarily! I have had a panel interview before and I was a little nervous but everyone else who was interviewed would have been nervous too and the panel are expecting that. ***However, as long as you are yourself and comfortable, then if the job or place is meant to be yours, it will be. If not, it won't.*** **Sometimes courses and jobs don't suit us and it is as important to know what we don't want as to know what we do. If you just do your best, you can't do any more than that. You may feel nervous, that is ok! Please don't beat yourself up for beating yourself up; mental double-edged clubs are no good. If you feel bad or nervous before or during the interview, that is ok; accept it (then it usually lessens). Just think about how good you will feel after the interview is done. Just be yourself, that is always enough,** ***no matter what you are doing in your life*** **and if we make mistakes, they are great, as they teach us something about the next time we are in the same situation."**

I wish you every success in all your interviews to come and I hope and know that the advice above can help.

Very best wishes for your examinations!

Thank you for purchasing this book,

Joseph

Printed in Great Britain
by Amazon

44286092R00031